Centuries of St. Louis

Centuries of St. Louis

By William Barnaby Faherty, S.J.

REEDY PRESS

St. Louis, Missouri

Dedicated to Wallace and Marie Hoffman

This book is printed on acid-free paper. ∞

Library of Congress Control Number: 2006940117

ISBN: 978-1-933370-06-4
        1-933370-06-8

Published by
Reedy Press
PO Box 5131
St. Louis, MO 63139, USA

For all information on all Reedy Press publications visit our website at www.reedypress.com.

Printed in the United States of America
07 08 09 10 11   5 4 3 2 1

design by Robyn Morgan

Contents

Introduction

Close to fifty years ago, while on the staff of the *Queen's Work* magazine, I had the pleasant task of interviewing prominent Catholic authors for the February *Catholic Press Month* feature. In that year, Paul Horgan had just won the Pulitzer Prize in history for *The Great River, the Rio Grande, in North American History*.

He had already won the Harper's Prize for a novel. The networks often carried his play "One Red Rose for Christmas" in preparation for the feast. He published a short novel, *Death in the Desert*. He told the fascinating story of Santa Fe, not in chronological narrative but through the eyes of fictional or historical individuals. He called it *Centuries of Santa Fe*. He later won a second Pulitzer in history with *Lamy*, the story of the first archbishop of Santa Fe.

I met Paul Horgan by arrangement at the train depot in Albuquerque. Unlike other transplanted easterners, he wore no southwestern garb. His appearance reminded me of a visit a few years ago to St. Louis of the Lord Mayor of Dublin. Among other questions, I asked how he decided what form of writing he used in each presentation. "I analyze my potential audience and my subject matter," he responded, "then I ask, 'how can I bring this material to that audience? ...'"

Horgan's answer guided me in writing this book. Almost thirty years ago, I was asked to write a pictorial history, *St. Louis Portrait*, which sold out immediately and was not republished. A few years later, Jack Walsh, head of the Convention and Visitors Bureau, asked me to do a pocket-size book on the city. Neighborhood historian NiNi Harris helped me with this book, as she had done with the earlier one. It is now in its fourth printing, with sales in the bestseller class. Both of these books were in straight narrative. The smaller book contained no pictures except those of the author and co-author.

With the market open for another book on St. Louis, I turned to Paul Horgan's example in *Centuries of Santa Fe*, with one difference. I used only real-life characters and sought to cover all groups of St. Louisans. Not all those chosen were famous individuals you may have heard about, but they were involved in interesting times and reflected those times. They were achievers, not celebrities, individuals of influence.

In reading this book, one may ask: "Why this selected participant?" before readily naming a more influential individual in that period. But significance did not always determine choice. Often areas of interest and diverse backgrounds determined the person. Above all, the choices gave balance and led to wide coverage of events.

Centuries of St. Louis

Commandant Louis St.Ange de Bellerive leaving Fort Chartres to cross the Mississippi and take up his headquarters in St. Louis. (photo by Captain William McKnight, reenactor)

Louis St. Ange
de Bellerive

First Commandant

The first French official in early St. Louis, Louis St. Ange de Bellerive, had come to the mid-continent with his father in 1720 from his birthplace in Canada. The elder Bellerive was given command of Fort Chartres, the rock-walled stronghold of the French in the Mississippi Valley, on the east bank of the river twenty miles above the mouth of the Kaskaskia River. On one occasion, the elder Bellerive led French troops and Illinois allies against the Fox warriors who had been harassing the peaceful Illinois people. King Louis XV recognized his achievements.

By the time of the French surrender at the end of the French and Indian War, the elder Bellerive had died and an officer by the name of Neyon de Villiers succeeded him. De Villiers determined to move to lower Louisiana, and many settlers from a village near Fort Chartres moved

4 Centuries of St. Louis

with him. The younger Bellerive, then officer in charge of the French troops at Vincennes on the Wabash, succeeded him.

Pontiac, chief of the Ottawa, came to Fort Chartres to ask his comrade in arms Bellerive to lead the tribes and continue the war with England. Pontiac's offer flattered him, but practical man that he was, he knew France's day was over. Britain controlled the seas. The French could provide few supplies, while the British could send well-equipped Scot and Irish regiments, even Hessian mercenaries, to fight their wars. St. Ange counseled peace. The disappointed chief carried on the fight for two years, holding the British back.

When the Black Watch, a Scots regiment, arrived at Fort Chartres, coming down the Ohio River and up the Mississippi, St. Ange turned over control of the fort to the British officer. At the orders of the Council in New Orleans, he took up his headquarters as commandant of the Territory at Pierre Laclede's newly opened trading post of St. Louis on the west bank of the river, forty miles upstream. Many French, mistreated by the British, went with him then or shortly after, making the trading post a village, now under Spanish rule.

Chief Pontiac visited him in 1769. Against the advice of St. Ange, the chief crossed the river to see longstanding friends. At the village of Cahokia, a renegade, presumably hired by a British trader, killed Pontiac. When St. Ange heard the news, he sent a contingent of troops across the river to bring Pontiac's body back to St. Louis. He gave the chief a full military funeral as an ally of the French in the French and Indian War. Nothing in the annals of English America rivaled it. It was the first significant funeral in early St. Louis history.

Few men in the years ahead would ever take leadership in St. Louis with the experience and background that this French-Canadian frontiersman possessed. He approved the name of the village St. Louis, chosen in honor of Louis XV's favorite saint, King Louis IX. He set up the Custom of Paris, the most liberal of all French codes, which created a climate of popular participation in local government. He gave titles to the home sites that Laclede had allotted to the inhabitants.

When the first lieutenant governor under Spain, Pedro Piernas, arrived in 1770, St. Ange welcomed him and accepted his offer of a captaincy in the Spanish service. Piernas followed St. Ange's advice on Indian affairs and ratified what he had done in his four years. The Spaniard renewed the privileges of the traders on the Missouri and generally let townsfolk run their own village. He did order them to build a church in the block set aside for it and invited the pastor of Kaskaskia, Canadian-born Father Pierre Gibault, to come up the river and bless it in June 1770. The first resident pastor, a Capuchin Franciscan from the Rhineland, Rev. Bernard Limpach, arrived in May six years later in time to bless a more substantial church on the same site. During twelve years, he served all the people, baptizing 410 Whites, 106 Blacks, and 92 Indians.

Bellerive's funeral in December 1774 was the second important funeral in early St. Louis. He left money for Masses for the repose of his soul. He was St. Louis's first leader, and in many ways one of its greatest. It had been his destiny to preside at the lowering of the Lilies of France from the flagstaff at Fort Chartres on the east bank of the Mississippi, and at the last outpost of a once great colonial empire on the west bank of the mighty stream. He handled each ceremony with dignity.

Reenactment of Margaret Blondeau Guion LeCompte, the first woman to live in St. Louis, with her second son, the first child born in St. Louis. (photo by Captain William McKnight)

Marguerite Blondeau Guion LeCompte

The Pioneer St. Louis Woman and Mother

Marguerite Blondeau, daughter of Thomas Blondeau and Marguerite Duclos, was born in Montreal. Like so many French Canadians, she came with her parents to the area of Fort Chartres in the early 1760s. She married Amable Guion, a stone mason, born at Fort Chartres, who had signed up to work with Laclede when the merchant-trader began his trading post in February 1764. Marguerite stayed at Cahokia with Amable, Jr., until May of that year. In spring, floods threatened Cahokia. Pregnant Marguerite and her parents came across the river. Eventually, housing became adequate. According to historian Dr. Fred Hodes, her son, Jean Baptiste Guion, was the first child born in St. Louis. With few stone masons in the area, her husband, Amable, had little trouble finding work. Several of the houses were of stone but most needed stonework for foundations and fireplaces.

Marguerite arrived before Laclede laid out the village, and she remembered that a young lad, Auguste Chouteau, four years younger than she was, carried the equipment Laclede used in laying out the plots. An early map shows the Guions in the second plot south of the *Place d'Armes*, the central square. Bellerive granted this plot to Marguerite's father, Thomas Blondeau, in 1766. The village stretched along the river rather than up-terrace to the west. Father Pierre Gibault, a fellow French Canadian, came over from his parish of Kaskaskia, Illinois, for the first Mass in St. Louis. She remembered him well. Father Bernard de Limpach, a German Capuchin, became the first pastor. There had been no slavery in Canada, but there were slaves in St. Louis. Marguerite slowly became used to the idea. But it did not seem to be a major factor in life in St. Louis. When the Spanish governor came, he forbade Indian slavery.

Far to the east, at that time the English colonists had revolted from the mother country. By 1780 Britain was ready to surround the American colonies and squeeze the people into submission. The British King, however, had not counted on France and even Spain giving support to the colonies in revolting. With the Spanish rule in St. Louis, the British decided to surround the entire western country with an attack from the south and from the north. The Spanish authorities in New Orleans forestalled trouble there. In 1780 the British sent northern tribes to attack St. Louis. Among the fourteen white men killed in the attack was Amable Guion. Father Bernard buried his body in the church lot. That winter, the lieutenant governor in St. Louis sent an expedition along with Illinois militia men and Potawatomi allies to attack a British base near Lake Michigan and capture supplies intended for a spring attack. The St. Louis militia succeeded without the loss of a man. The following year, Britain made peace.

On August 24, 1784, Marguerite Blondeau married Guillaume LeCompte, who had come from Quebec and ran a quarry. Laclede had died bankrupt in 1788. Auguste Chouteau took over his business interests. He married Therese, the daughter of Gabriel Cerre, a merchant from Kaskaskia and the richest man in the area. Chouteau's half brother and half sisters married prominent St. Louisans, Pelangie Kiersereau, Joseph Papin, Charles Gratiot, and Sylvester Labadie. Auguste and his brother, Pierre, prospered in the Osage trade in the 1790s, the days of Governor Zenon Trudeau. Trudeau, a native of New Orleans, also urged local traders to go up the Missouri and find a waterway to the Pacific. Baron de Carondelet, governor in New Orleans, offered a reward for the successful explorer.

Marguerite Blondeau knew that her fellow French Canadians traveled widely and had gone far into the northern interior. In the meantime, she would not have been surprised if one might have reached the Pacific. But all St. Louisans were surprised when a wandering Frenchman, Pierre Vial, whose daughter Marie married Benjamin Verger that very year in Florissant, reached St. Louis with a commission from the lieutenant governor in Santa Fe. Vial earlier had gone from San Antonio to the capital of New Mexico twice. The authorities previously had no clear vision of the distance between these centers of the Spanish Empire. He returned from St. Louis to Santa Fe a year later.

As king of the largest empire in the world, one might have presumed that King Charles IV of Spain would have little time to be aware of English-speaking newcomers to the Louisiana Territory from the American state of Maryland, or that his colonial troops included many Irish. But he was aware and sent a priest from Dublin, James Maxwell, trained in Salamanca in Spain, to Upper Louisiana as religious leader. He took up residence near Ste. Genevieve and regularly visited St. Louis. When he did, Marguerite attended his Masses.

In the meantime, Napoleon became ruler of France and hoped to restore its empire overseas. But the British victory over the French at Trafalgar ended that dream. He had gained Louisiana Territory in a secret treaty with Spain. Now he sold it to the young Republic of the United States for three dollars an acre.

People came to call the day of the ceremony of transfer of the Upper Louisiana Territory from Spain to France to the United States in the spring of 1804 as the "Day of Three Flags." Marguerite remembered that the ceremony spread over two days. The flag of Spain went down on the ninth of March. The tri-color of France went up for one night. It came down the next morning, and the Stars and Stripes rose. A conciliatory man, Captain Amos Stoddard, was in charge. President Thomas Jefferson sent a French-born member of Congress from Pennsylvania, Jean Baptiste Lucas, to be judge of land claims and a focal point of antislavery forces. But the proslavery wealthy French prevailed.

Missouri became a distinct territory with its center in St. Louis. The French residents were able to keep their joyful Sunday observances over the years in face of attempts by some newcoming Anglo-Americans to introduce the gloomy, Puritanical Sabbath of New England. But the French lost out in the struggle to keep the conciliatory legal procedures in the face of Anglo-American ways that seemed to them to create hostility. The Custom of Paris they lived under gave more consideration to family ties, to the rights of widows, and to community concerns than English common law, but the latter prevailed.

In the meantime, Lewis and Clark had gone up the Missouri, crossed the mountains to the Columbia River and Pacific Ocean, and a year later returned in triumph to St. Louis. Anglo-

Americans from the east and Irish, Protestant and Catholic, from the old country came—not in great numbers, but skilled in merchandising—and St. Louis was becoming the merchandise center of the entire Mississippi Valley. Guillaume LeCompte died in February 1809. He left his estate of $5,000 to his wife, Marguerite. They had had no children.

Many priests of old Louisiana Territory who had come during the Spanish regime and were sponsored by the government left for Spanish territory in Cuba or Mexico. Not Father Maxwell! He liked Missouri and had received a grant of land for an Irish colony. Unfortunately, that did not come to be because of the Napoleonic Wars. He saw the great need for an English-speaking priest and stayed. President James Madison named Maxwell a member of the first Territorial Legislature of Upper Louisiana in 1812. His fellow members chose him first president. Unfortunately, he died in a fall from his horse within a year.

Marguerite welcomed the arrival of Joseph Charless, a Welshman, who started the first newspaper in St. Louis, the *Missouri Republican*. Many Irish and Anglo-Americans settled in St. Louis. Marguerite was among those confirmed by Bishop Joseph Benedict Flaget of Kentucky in late 1814. He came, with a welcome from Governor William Clark, to look over the area spiritually in the name of the new bishop of the Louisiana Territory, Louis William Valentine

DuBourg. Flaget found religion in St. Louis at a low ebb and wondered if Ste. Genevieve might not be a better residence for the new bishop.

In 1818 Bishop Louis W. V. DuBourg chose to move to St. Louis. He was not at home in the anti-clerical spirit of New Orleans. French anticlericalism never touched the French in St. Louis, just as the Puritanical spirit of New England never cut the joy of the St. Louis French. Marguerite Blondeau recognized the great value of Bishop DuBourg's bringing so many prominent religious people to the area: Mother Philippine Duchesne; the Vincentian Fathers, led by Father D'Andreis, assisted by Father Joseph Rosati—brilliant men from Italy; and, a few years later, Jesuit missionaries from Belgium, led by Father Charles Felix van Quickenborne, who started their seminary in Florissant. Marguerite pledged her share to Bishop DuBourg's new brick "cathedral."

A priest who came with Bishop DuBourg, Father Francis Neil, opened St. Louis Academy, which two years later became St. Louis College. At the same time, girls could go to Mother Duchesne's school, at first in St. Charles and then after two years in Florissant.

The last great political event that Marguerite Blondeau witnessed was the admission of Missouri into the Union as a slave state. Actually, the decision to allow slavery in Missouri had been settled in the territorial days, when Jefferson's hopes for free soil lost.

In 1823 a group of Belgian Jesuit missionaries arrived in St. Louis after trekking across southern Illinois from the Ohio River village of Shawneetown. The following year, with a promise of a subsidy from the government of President James Monroe, they began an Indian school at Florissant on a farm Bishop DuBourg had given them.

At the time, Judge Wilson Primm set out to tell the story of the founding of St. Louis. The Chouteau family claimed that Auguste was cofounder of St. Louis. He apparently did nothing to dispel this rumor. Primm interviewed several early residents, including Madame LeCompte. She was described as having "a happy facility of language and manner, united with a spirit of politeness." Even though blind and almost bed-ridden, she recalled the events of the past that she had witnessed. Among them was the fact that Auguste Chouteau had been four years younger than she at the time of her coming from Cahokia. She remembered that he carried the chain when Laclede laid out the village. That indicated that Auguste was fourteen years of age at the time. In spite of Marguerite's testimony and that of others, the Chouteaus continued the false claim.

Bishop DuBourg returned to France, and Joseph Rosati became Bishop of St. Louis in 1827. He brought the Jesuits from Florissant to man the small college begun by Father Neil that had continued with uncertain steps. The school won a university charter from the state of Missouri in

1831. With the aid of businessman John Mullanphy, Mother Duchesne moved her school from Florissant to St. Louis.

In 1829 Auguste Chouteau died. Marguerite outlived him. Her last public act was a donation for the Cathedral on the waterfront. She died in October 1832 and was buried in the Cathedral lot on the Eve of All Saints.

Marguerite Blondeau Guion LeCompte had seen memorable events. She was a participant in the development of one of the nation's great cities. She had seen the last settlement of the French Empire in America grow from a French trading post to a prosperous and peaceful French, Irish, and Anglo-American community, the merchandise center of the mid-continent.

John Mullanphy (David Lossos)

John Mullanphy
and John O'Fallon

Generous Merchants

In his book *Personal Recollections*, Mayor John
Fletcher Darby selected for special mention two
of the great men whom he knew personally in
American St. Louis: John Mullanphy in the early
American years, and John O'Fallon in the 1820s and
1830s. The reader of Darby's book readily concludes
that these two superior citizens left St. Louis a much
better place for having chosen it as their home.

A native of Ireland, Mullanphy had spent some
time in France before coming to the Mississippi
Valley shortly after the Louisiana Purchase. A man of
energy, foresight and judgment, he purchased
extensive property in St. Louis and the Florissant
Valley. The fact that he spoke French gave him great
opportunities in business and in public service. He
opened stores in St. Louis and in Natchez, Mississippi.
He built many houses and served as a director of the
Branch Bank of the United States. He became Justice
of the Peace and frequently served as alderman.

He contributed to the Cathedral. He helped the Daughters of Charity open the first hospital in the West, and he assisted Mother Duchesne in moving her school from Florissant to a site in St. Louis City. A Jesuit missionary alleged that he paid the entire cost of St. Ferdinand's Church in Florissant. Besides these major public gifts, Mullanphy provided help to the poor in many ways. When Daniel D. Page operated the only baker's shop in town, Mullanphy left several hundred dollars with him to provide bread for poor and indigent families. He left five hundred dollars in his will to each American Catholic bishop to aid orphans in his diocese.

A man of strong prejudices, he was most tenacious of his rights. He told Mayor Darby frequently that he would spend one thousand dollars before he would be cheated or defrauded of one dollar. He carried this concern to amazing limits, yet much of his wealth went to benevolent purposes.

He sent his daughters to the Ursuline Convent in New Orleans for education, and then to France. His son, Bryan, studied in France and England. All the daughters, except one who planned to enter a convent, married prominent men, usually military officers serving at Jefferson Barracks. Their descendants include a surprising number of well-known St. Louis families.

"At the time of his death," Darby asserted, "John Mullanphy was said to be the wealthiest man in the Valley of the Mississippi, his estate being reckoned by millions." Convinced that his son, Bryan, later mayor of St. Louis and a judge, was irresponsible in his use of money, Mullanphy left the son out of his will. When their father died in 1833, the six daughters gave Bryan one-seventh of their shares. Bryan's portion amounted to half a million dollars.

Bryan never married. He left much of his fortune for immigrants from Ireland. It was the fifth Irish help organization in the records of St. Louis. Bryan's money provided for the Mullanphy Emigrant Home. Eventually, his estate supported Travelers' Aid. For many years, the hospital under the care of the Daughters of Charity bore the name Mullanphy Hospital.

John O'Fallon was similarly successful and equally generous, but more easygoing and carefree in his giving. While St. Louisans had great respect for out-standing individuals, O'Fallon also gained their love and affection. Contemporaries praised the manner, grace, and single-hearted purpose in every donation.

John's father, Dr. James O'Fallon, of County Athlone in Ireland, had served as a surgeon in Washington's army during the Revolutionary War. The senior O'Fallon then moved to Louisville, Kentucky, where he met and married Frances Clark, sister of Generals George Rogers Clark and William Clark, army officer destined to be famous.

In youth, John O'Fallon served in the Indian Wars and in the War of 1812. After his military career, he came to St. Louis, where his uncle William was Indian agent. John prospered in partnership with Alexander McNair and James Kennerly as a supplier for various

John O'Fallon (Saint Louis University)

army posts in the West. O'Fallon invested his newly acquired wealth in many local enterprises. He was president of the Branch Bank of the United States and one of the promoters of the Pacific and other railroads, such as the Ohio and Mississippi and the North Missouri. He was the first president of each of the early banks in St. Louis.

O'Fallon helped his Episcopal church and built a Methodist church at the northwest corner of Fourth Street and Washington for his wife's congregation. He put up two Federal-style buildings on Spruce Street for the medical college of Saint Louis University, where his son-in-law, Dr. Charles Alexander Pope, was dean. Later he built the O'Fallon Technical Institute, the forerunner of the Engineering School of Washington University.

John Darby spoke of him in this vein: "He was, beyond all doubt, the most open-handed and liberal man the City of St. Louis has ever produced, a leader in every noble undertaking, and the foremost and largest contributor in every public enterprise. He sprang to every businessman's assistance without waiting to be called upon. He has done more to assist the merchants and businessmen of St. Louis than any man who ever lived in this town. . . . When any of his friends were appointed to public office, requiring bonds to be given, he did not wait to be asked. . . ."

O'Fallon built a mansion on his estate called Athlone on the terrace above the Mississippi River at the north end of St. Louis. The city would purchase it years later and create a public park named in honor of the family.

John Baptist Druyts (Midwest Jesuit Archives)

Father John Baptist Druyts

Eminent Educator

U nlike those two civic leaders, John Mullanphy and John O'Fallon, whose names adorn streets and schools even today, Father John Baptist Druyts was little known even among his contemporaries in St. Louis. Yet he taught at Saint Louis University during one of the most prestigious periods in its long history. From the age of twenty-four until his untimely death in 1861 at the age of fifty, Druyts rarely left Saint Louis University.

He was ordained to the priesthood by Bishop Peter Richard Kenrick in 1843. Unlike his Belgian colleagues, Fathers de Smet and Verhaegen, he never engaged in preaching or missionary work. His life centered on the school, first as professor, then Prefect of Studies.

When he came to Saint Louis University, the school stood on the highest plateau in its early history. The first university chartered west of the

Mississippi, it boasted a fine medical school with a distinguished faculty and a program in law under the leadership of Judge Richard A. Buckner. Several of its first graduates were to win acclaim in public life. Father James O. Van de Velde, S.J., a linguist and financier, directed the school at the time.

Father George Carroll, a native of Maryland, followed Van de Velde. He was one of the first Americans to join the predominantly Belgian Jesuits in the Midwest. Shortly, he and Van de Velde became bishops of the Church, he in Covington, Kentucky, Van de Velde in Chicago.

Druyts became president of Saint Louis University in 1847—a steady, inconspicuous, friendly man, he could easily have been passed over in the selection of presidents for Saint Louis University. Fortunately, he was not. His equanimity and good nature were evident on the freezing winter days and in the ninety-degree heat of summer, no less than in the heaven-lovely springs and falls along the Mississippi. During his years as president of the university, St. Louis became an archdiocese, the second in the United States, before New York, or Philadelphia, or even New Orleans, that had a Spanish bishop in colonial days. In letters to bishops in Bavaria and Austria, St. Louis Archbishop P. R. Kenrick pointed out that St. Louis was the best place for Catholics in America. He welcomed immigrants from all countries. Several of these immigrants joined the faculty of Saint Louis University, and some enrolled as students.

At the beginning of May 1849, the Asiatic cholera hit St. Louis. All boarders at Saint Louis University who stayed on the campus survived. Several who went home died. In the midst of the cholera epidemic, another calamity struck the city. In May 1849, a fire broke out among the steamboats lined up at the levee. Eventually, twenty-seven boats burst into flames. The flames spread to business houses but did not reach the university or the cathedral. Before it was brought under control, the fire destroyed four hundred buildings in fifteen blocks and twenty-four steamboats at the levee.

After these disasters, the City of St. Louis saw a period of growth and prosperity. Houses lined Fourth Street from Market ten or twelve blocks north. Residences were growing up on Fifth and Sixth Streets and on all east-west streets from Market to Locust, an area southwest of the university campus. There was as yet little improvement west of Tenth Street, but the trend of the city development had obviously turned from north-south, stretching along the river to crowning the terraces to the west. The Planters House, St. Louis's first and finest hotel, was six years old. The new courthouse had begun construction the previous year. The first railroad was soon to move west from the city up the Mill Creek Valley, once Chouteau Pond was drained.

As the City of St. Louis moved ahead, so did the university under the leadership of Father Druyts. He divided the student body into two groups, with separate "rec" areas, dining rooms, study halls, and classrooms, as well as distinct religious and educational programs. This formed the later division between Saint Louis University and St. Louis University High School.

John Lesperance, a Canadian writer who remembered Father Druyts from his years as a student in St. Louis, spoke of him as "eminently practical, a financier, a builder, and a skillful administrator generally." Father Druyts's virtues, he said, were heroic: "He was a saint, single-minded, utterly without guile, unconventional, firm as a monolith when there was need, sweet as summer. He presented a combination of rare qualities which go to make up the exceptional among men."

A contemporary, Father Walter Hill, wrote of him: "No superior was ever more generally loved than was Father Druyts, a paragon of charity, prudence, and practical good sense." A later historian of the Missouri Province, Father Gilbert Garraghan, wrote years later, "Everywhere through the records and correspondence of the day, there breathes a uniform esteem and reverence for the personality of Father Druyts."

After the Mexican War (1846), more Latin-American students, especially from New Mexico, came to St. Louis for education. The first two territorial delegates of the New Mexico Territory, Mariano and Miguel Otero, were among these students at Saint Louis University. During those years, the Santa Fe Trail brought wealth into the growing city.

As a result of the revolutions in Europe in 1848, Saint Louis University inherited a School of Philosophy and Theology, with an entire faculty of three professors and sixteen seminarians from the Upper German Province, called the Swiss Province. The Jesuits hurried up the completion of the rock building at Florissant on Seminary Ridge above Florissant to house some of these students.

The middle '50s of the century presented the first split among the people of St. Louis. A group of nativists, hostile to all immigrants, threatened the university, but were thwarted by Father Druyts. Presumably, he walked up and down in front of St. Francis Xavier Church reciting the Psalms. Be that as it may, while the "Know-Nothing" rioters, so-called because whenever asked what they stood for, they always knew "nothing," turned on the Saint Louis University School of Medicine. The two buildings, gifts of John O'Fallon, whose son-in-law, Dr. Charles A. Pope, was dean, were in danger. Father Druyts said flatly, "We own the charter. If you doctors want to leave, we'll get new doctors." So they did not move at that time.

In the meantime, the Know-Nothings showed their true colors. While they opposed Lutherans as well as Catholics, they welcomed the anti-Church

"Forty-Eighter" Germans. These Germans had hoped to unite their country under a liberal constitution, but failed, and came to the United States. Anticlerical in Europe, they interpreted the American scene in European terms. They met a wall, steady, quiet John Baptist Druyts, who lived his life in American terms and promoted American values.

Two years later, in the election year of 1854, the Know-Nothings threatened the medical buildings again. By this time, a genial St. Louisan, Father John Verdin, had succeeded Father Druyts, who had become superior of the Missouri Jesuits. The medical school separated from the university, to the disadvantage of both. Several years later, the Know-Nothings followed a quieter path as members of a new political party, the Republicans.

Shortly after, a group of St. Louisans led by Dr. William Greenleaf Eliot, a member of the original board of trustees of the Saint Louis University Medical School, began "Eliot Seminary." A few years later it took the name of Washington University. John O'Fallon started O'Fallon Technical Institute there, a forerunner of Washington University's Engineering School.

In the meantime, several hundred more German immigrants had come to Missouri. Like the Catholics and Evangelicals before them, they were devout churchgoers and were to have a positive and more lasting influence on the area than the secularist "Forty-Eighters." One hundred

founded Trinity Lutheran Church in Soulard under
the leadership of Otto C. F. Walther, who had
studied theology at the University of Leipzig and
had begun the first parish school in St. Louis. A
larger group settled in southeast Missouri. They
began a seminary. It moved to St. Louis in 1849
and eventually gained the name of Concordia
Seminary, the center of the largest and most con-
servative Lutheran synod in America. A century
later, Dr. Walter Maier of Concordia Seminary
became the "Voice of the Lutheran Hour" on radio,
originating on Station KFUO in St. Louis.

Henry Shaw (Missouri Botanical Garden)

Henry Shaw

Private Person, Public Donor

An immigrant of England at the age of eighteen, merchant Henry Shaw succeeded in business as did John Mullanphy and John O'Fallon. Like them, he left future generations indebted for his legacies. But while they were visible, outgoing Irish personalities, he seemed an uptight Englishman to his fellow St. Louisans.

Eighteen-year-old Henry came to Canada with his father, Joseph Shaw, in 1818. He had completed the classical course at Mill Hill School near London. His father had been a successful businessman from Sheffield, England. Actually, the senior Shaw owed a considerable amount of money to his sister's relatives. He had partnered with an American who didn't keep his agreement to sell in the States the Sheffield ware that Joseph Shaw had provided. Henry's mother, in contrast, came from a financially and socially established family. His maternal uncles worked with him over the years. One manufactured cutlery in Sheffield that Henry marketed in

St. Louis. The other handled Henry's shipping in London.

Henry located his father's cutlery in New Orleans but found that the old French city was not a center of trade at the time. So he moved to St. Louis with his merchandise. At the time, enterprising young St. Louisans wanted to gain wealth on the Santa Fe Trail. Henry was content to sit at his desk and keep careful accounts, even the names of the steamboats that brought his materials to St. Louis. He opened a store and brought materials inexpensively from England to New Orleans up to St. Louis by water.

When he came to St. Louis, he didn't like the place, in winter or in summer. He said he would rather live anywhere under the British government, even in the most distant and unregulated colony England possessed, than in these free American States. And yet, he stayed and influenced the St. Louis community in a distinct way.

Shaw's shipment of goods from England showed a constantly expanding variety of merchandise—at first cutlery from Sheffield, then hinges, locks, shovels, tongs, springbolts, nails, and padlocks. A summer shipment included two categories of commodities, tableware from London and a wide variety of cutting tools from Sheffield. He never paid in cash. Instead, he shipped American products that would bring good prices in England, hemp, cotton, tobacco. So he made money both shipping and receiving.

He prevailed upon his mother and sisters to leave England. He brought them to upstate New York, where his father, Joseph Shaw, had located. At that juncture, Joseph Shaw's brother-in-law hired a lawyer to push for the money Joseph Shaw owed. Eventually, Henry paid his father's debts. By 1829 Henry Shaw had amassed a fortune that totaled nearly a quarter of a million dollars. His profits in that one year had come to $22,876.34. The often-repeated myth that he thought he had made enough money and was getting out of business does not give the full economic picture. While cutlery from Sheffield and goods from the neighboring places in England still sold, canals and railroads were making it easier for firms on the Atlantic seaboard to move their products into the interior. The northeastern states were pushing for higher tariffs on imports. As a result, domestic manufacturers could now compete effectively with imported ware. So Shaw turned to amassing property in the southwestern section of St. Louis and beyond.

Shaw did little socializing and never married. He took little part in civic affairs and almost nothing in the political arena. He did own slaves, eventually as many as fifteen. But before the time of the Emancipation Proclamation, he freed them. He did not appear to be close to anyone, except over the years he had great concern for his protégé, Joseph Monell. He visited Joseph when he was in the orphanage, and put him through elementary school, Smith Academy, and Washington University.

As time went on, Shaw gave thought to what he might do with the acres that he had picked up in the southwest section of St. Louis, especially the area around his country home. During the Civil War, leaders of the city thought of opening a park but they did not succeed in pushing it through. So, at the suggestion of a friend, Dr. Thomas O'Reilly, Shaw started Tower Grove Park. It stretched east and west fifteen blocks from Grand Boulevard to Kingshighway and north and south four blocks from Arsenal to Magnolia. He later recruited a fellow Englishman, James Gurney, to manage the park.

In the meantime, on a visit to Chatsworth, the estate of the "Bachelor Duke" in England, he had been impressed by the garden. He came home with the idea of establishing a garden in St. Louis on a large section of his property north of the park and west of Tower Grove Avenue. With the advice of Dr. George Engleman, an amateur naturalist and a practicing gynecologist, Shaw was able to purchase the Leipzig Conservatory botanical materials.

With the assistance and advice then of Sir William Jackson Hooker, director of the Gardens at Kew, near London, England, of Dr. Engleman in St. Louis, and Dr. Asa Gray at Harvard, the out-standing American academic botanist, he began the garden. Director Hooker called Shaw's proposal "a gift to glory in." Shaw spent the next twenty years overseeing his city properties and investments, reading and writing history, and taking care of his Garden that steadily gained popularity among his grateful fellow citizens.

Archbishop Peter Richard Kenrick

Archbishop Peter Richard Kenrick

Shepherd of Mid-America

D ublin-born Peter Richard Kenrick, a graduate of Maynooth, the leading seminary in English-speaking lands, was ordained a priest in March 1832, at the age of twenty-six. He was teaching seminarians in Dublin a year later, when his brother, Bishop Francis Patrick of Philadelphia, asked him to come to America. This he did in 1833. Though a scholar by inclination, he succeeded in various aspects of Church ministry.

By 1841 in the Mississippi Valley, Bishop Joseph Rosati of St. Louis had labored for over twenty years. He had promoted education by chartering a college in Perryville, Missouri; by inviting Mother Duchesne and Belgian Jesuits who had opened schools for whites and Indians in Florissant to take over schools in St. Louis; and a decade later, by encouraging the Sisters of St. Joseph to teach deaf in Carondelet. He began a cathedral near the waterfront. He welcomed Mercy Sisters in healthcare and the

Visitations to open an academy. In 1841 he sought the assistance of Father Peter Richard Kenrick, whom Pope Gregory XVI appointed Coadjutor Bishop of St. Louis. When Rosati died two years later, Kenrick succeeded him.

Mayor John Darby described the new bishop as "a learned and finished scholar . . . a man of great erudition, pious, modest and unobtrusive, meek and unostentatious in manner, he seems to have devoted himself to his sacred and holy calling with a singleness and steadiness of purpose that few men have ever surpassed." He became archbishop in 1847. Historian Thomas Scharf called him "one of the most distinguished prelates of the American Church, a learned theologian, an able administrator, and a man of greatest generosity and benevolence." Like Rosati, he gained recognition as one of the outstanding bishops in Christendom.

Newcomers from Europe came to recognize Kenrick as the "Father of Immigrants." He understood their varied backgrounds and accepted their diverse languages. He encouraged gradual Americanization. He wanted bishops who spoke German in those areas where many German Catholics lived, such as Quincy, Illinois. Archbishop Kenrick also showed his great concern for the poor in St. Louis, immigrant and native, by encouraging young Father Ambrose Heim, who started and successfully ran a "People's Bank." To increase the number of poor people using this forerunner of the modern credit union, the archbishop moved Father Heim to the Cathedral and opened membership to all the city's people. After Father Heim's premature death, Kenrick ran the day-to-day affairs of the highly successful bank.

Archbishop Kenrick saw St. Louis grow from 16,000 when he came in the 1840s to 77,860 ten years later, and to 160,773 in 1860. Commerce and industry grew. The people prospered. The Santa Fe Trail continued to bring wealth to St. Louis and needed goods to New Mexico and Mexico, generally on the wagons made by Joseph Murphy, one of Archbishop Kenrick's flock in St. Louis.

An advocate of peace, Kenrick saw hostility begin to grow. While a slave state, Missouri had so many non-slave economic interests that the state was neither secessionist nor abolitionist. Alone of all the states in the Union, Missouri stayed with the Democrat nominee, the conciliatory Senator Stephen Douglas. After Lincoln's election in 1860, several states of the Deep South seceded from the Union. On March 4, 1861, the day of Lincoln's inaugural address, Archbishop Kenrick sent a pastoral letter to his people. He counseled them to be aware of aggressive action by individuals and groups not recognized by law.

Military forces of the seceding states fired on Fort Sumter in April. Lincoln called for volunteers to save the Union. Kenrick called for calm. Since the War Between the States was for a political goal, the saving of the Union, Kenrick sought to call for peace, as Pope Pius IX recommended in letters to the archbishops of New York and New Orleans.

William Greenleaf Eliot (Missouri Historical Society)

William Greenleaf Eliot

Religious and Civic Leader

Although outside of St. Louis, William Greenleaf Eliot may be most recognized as the grandfather of the great poet T. S. Eliot, Dr. Eliot's role as religious, civic, and community leader in St. Louis had a profound effect on the community.

A graduate of the Harvard Divinity School in 1834, Eliot founded the first Unitarian church west of the Mississippi River in St. Louis that same year. While serving as minister of the First Unitarian Church for more than thirty-five years, Eliot's humanitarian spirit was instrumental in the founding of many of St. Louis's proudest educational, charitable, and cultural institutions.

Most notably, in 1853, Eliot Seminary was established. Uneasy with the use of his name, Dr. Eliot quickly had the school's name changed to Washington University, in honor of the nation's first president. St. Louis now had two chartered university schools. Some of the supporters of

Saint Louis University, such as John O'Fallon, who had contributed two buildings to Saint Louis University's School of Medicine, turned his interest to the new school. He gave the O'Fallon Technical Institute, which eventually became the Washington University School of Engineering.

Washington University grew and the professors took an active part in the St. Louis movement of philosophy in the 1880s. In the meantime, Saint Louis University took a less visible St. Louis orientation and gave its attention to daughter institutions in other mid-western cities.

Eliot was instrumental in the establishment of elementary education in St. Louis as well. He co-founded Mary Institute—now a part of Mary Institute Country Day School—in memory of his daughter Mary, who died as a child. He also assisted in the development of the St. Louis Public School System.

A staunch abolitionist and women's rights supporter, Eliot was active as a philanthropist in the Civil War. He founded the Western Sanitary Commission, which established, equipped, and supplied military hospitals. Since fighting was widespread, the Commission established floating hospitals on steamboats that could better serve the wounded.

Eliot assisted with the establishment of a multitude of charities in St. Louis, including the

Colored Orphans Home, the Soldiers Orphans Home, and the American Missionary Society.

He was also an accomplished writer, focusing his works on the beliefs that meant most to him: theology, morality, and abolitionism. His most noted work is *The Story of Archer Alexander: From Slavery to Freedom*.

Ellen Ewing Sherman

Ellen Ewing Sherman

Wife of a Warrior

B y 1861 William Tecumseh Sherman had served his term in the military and presided over a streetcar line in St. Louis. When the states of the Deep South began to secede, General William Harney, commander of the Army in the West, worked out a plan of conciliation with former Governor Sterling Price, head of the state militia.

Congressman Frank Blair, however, prevailed upon Lincoln to call Harney to Washington and put a drastic New Englander, Captain Nathaniel Lyon, in charge of the federal troops at the arsenal in St. Louis. Lyon moved any military supplies that might have fallen into Southern hands to Union territory. The State Assembly voted to remain in the Union and businessmen saw no future in the Southern Confederacy that was forming. The great religious leader Archbishop Kenrick, as mentioned previously, called for calm.

General Daniel Frost, a Northerner and veteran of the Mexican War, had, as a member of the State Senate several years before, proposed a state militia as a safety belt between Northern and Southern extremists. He called the local unit of the state militia for its annual encampment at Lindell Grove at the west end of St. Louis. In response, Lyon called into federal service a great number of volunteers, three-fourths of them recent German immigrants who had not yet gotten involved in city affairs. Frost wisely surrendered to the overwhelming force. Unwisely, after some delay, Lyon marched his men and their prisoners through streets lined with spectators, including friends and relatives of the captured militiamen.

Among these spectators were two future Union generals, Ulysses S. Grant and William T. Sherman. Sherman's only comment about the event was that an intoxicated man had wanted to push through the Union lines and was stopped. He pulled out a gun and fired the first shot. A Union officer was shot, and some civilians and soldiers were killed or wounded in the retaliation. Rioting swept the city. Southern sympathizers fired on Home Guards, marching to Broadway and Walnut the next morning. Many pro-Southern families left the city for the country. In August Lyon faced Missouri, Arkansas, Texas, and Louisiana Confederates in Southwest Missouri, and he was killed. General John Fremont took charge in Missouri and was slow to act except that he freed the slaves. The next day, Lincoln cancelled the unauthorized action. Fremont did not come to the rescue of Colonel James Mulligan and his troops at Lexington in western Missouri, captured by Missouri Confederates under General Sterling Price.

In the meantime, General Sherman had predicted a long and terrible war. That brought only ridicule. His wife stood with him in this time as she did in so many other ways. She devoted her time to charitable activity, especially with the U.S. Sanitary Commission, a body organized to give material and spiritual help to soldiers during the war. Further, besides all the wounded who were brought by steamboat from Shiloh and other battles in the course of the war, many refugees came from turmoil outstate.

Hostilities disrupted business and social life. The Chamber of Commerce split into two factions and would not reunite until 1875. Federal authorities harassed the families of such Confederates as General Frost, who had gone South after he was paroled. But Grant then began to move South and, the Eads gunboats built in St. Louis became a major factor in his success in opening the Mississippi.

Sherman saw that the war would last long and predicted that ultimately supplies and movement rather than courage and bravery would win. While Grant and Lee killed men, Sherman destroyed supplies. His willingness to give a fair treatment to Johnson's Confederates who surrendered to him in North Carolina late in the conflict brought the charge of treason from Edwin Stanton, the Secretary of War. But in the end, it was the lack of supplies that forced Lee to surrender, not the many men whom Grant lost. Sherman had destroyed property, and people ridiculed him, but he brought an end to the war. His wife Ellen was a strong supporter at the time when few were with him in spirit.

Even before the end of the conflict, a Republican lawyer, Charles Drake, a vindictive member of the Missouri State Assembly who had opposed the reelection of Lincoln in 1864, maneuvered for political control of the state. At the Constitutional Convention of 1865 in St. Louis, he brought about the end of slavery in Missouri, but did little else that was good. He wanted restrictions on all but the most ultra-liberal whites. He required a special oath of clergymen, teachers, and lawyers. A young parish priest, Father John Cummings, had to appeal to the Supreme Court to preserve his right to preach to his people. He won his appeal, a landmark in civil liberties.

Industry continued to grow in St. Louis and by 1870 surpassed all-American communities except New York and Philadelphia in the number and value of manufacturing plants and production. Quarrying and brick building were strong. The brewery business changed from many small breweries to three or four large ones. In 1876 the city and the county separated and St. Louis got home rule—good in those days, but a proven disaster later on.

After the war, General Sherman might well have been elected president. Mrs. Sherman never begrudged her husband's refusal to run for the presidency. When the general's position in the Army brought him back to St. Louis as head of the Department of the West, a grateful citizenry gave the Shermans a fine home on Garrison Avenue, a few blocks north of Washington. The general was present at the dedication of Eads Bridge, another monument to the great man, James Buchanan Eads, who had built the gunboats that opened the Mississippi for Grant. While the Shermans resided in the city only off and on from 1850 to 1890, Ellen and the general cherished their home in St. Louis and insisted on being buried in Calvary Cemetery.

William Torrey Harris (Missouri Historical Society)

William Torrey Harris

Educational Philosopher

U p to the Civil War, thinkers and writers in St. Louis were religiously oriented, such as Archbishop Kenrick and Lutheran leader C. W. F. Walther. After the conflict, at an opposite position stood William Torrey Harris and his associates in the St. Louis Movement. This group included William Greenleaf Elliot, founder of Washington University, and Lieutenant Governor Henry Brockmeyer, who brought many European ideas with him to St. Louis. These men believed that the outlook on life of German philosopher George Wilhelm Hegel, 1770–1831, was the best way to promote an ideal democratic society.

In addition to being an educator, Harris published influential magazines. *The Journal of Speculative Philosophy* began in 1867 and continued for twenty-two years under his direction. Josiah Royce, William James, and John Dewey wrote for it. While religious leaders saw no conflict between faith and science, William Torrey Harris, though personally devout, held that in spirit and content, secular truth was hostile to religious truth. In his mind, religious education belonged exclusively in the church, a position antagonistic to the vast majority of schools in St. Louis. Most were under Catholic or Lutheran tutelage until his time. Harris's ideas gained wide acceptance in America and Australia. Australian schools imitated his secularistic pattern, rather than that of the religious-based educational pattern common to most of the British Commonwealth.

As an educational philosopher, Harris influenced people widely, both by word and policy. He did not believe that humans were basically good, as his Catholic neighbors did, but rather that by the use of their reason they could devise a system in which all chose to be good. Since the schools existed to prepare children for intelligent citizenship, no hint of vocational preparation was to intrude. Nor was religion, at any level. No educator in the United States stood higher than he in public and professional esteem. Eventually, he became United States Commissioner of Education.

While Superintendent of Public Education in St. Louis, he had introduced scientific and manual arts into the curriculum, started art and music education, and added the library as a normal part of school facilities. He made St. Louis schools a model for the nation and won acclaim as the Horace Mann of the last quarter of a century. Even though they disagreed with him basically in his views on religion, Harris hired many Catholic women of Irish ancestry to teach in his public schools. These teachers spoke with admiration of Dr. Harris. Lucy Schwienher, a teacher of Irish-German Catholic background, wrote her master's thesis on his work.

In 1872, with Harris's encouragement, Susan Blow, a local educator, went east to study with Maria Kraus-Bolte, an educational leader from Holland who had opened a private kindergarten in New York. After a year, Susan returned to St. Louis, where she and Harris designed a kindergarten program to bridge the gap between family and the primary school. Children would be taught punctuality, silence, obedience, and self-control. This would help them with their education later on.

Many prominent professors were among Harris's associates in the St. Louis Movement. Philosopher George H. Howison taught many young men who later accepted chairs of philosophy at various colleges and universities around the country. A big step forward came in 1891. The St. Louis College of Medicine, originally the School of Medicine of Saint Louis University, affiliated with Washington University. The following year, the first school of medicine to open in St. Louis, the Missouri Medical College, also joined with Washington University,

While these members of the St. Louis Movement looked upon Hegel as the greatest, wisest philosopher in the whole history of time—greater than Aristotle, Plato, Aquinas, Kant, Descartes, and others—a century later most St. Louisans would know little about Hegel, and fewer would have heard of the St. Louis Movement. Harris left his mark in education, not in philosophy.

John J. O'Neill

John J. O'Neill

Workingman's Legislator

State Legislator and four-time Congressman John J. O'Neill was born in St. Louis on June 25, 1846, when education for poor children was rare. At the age of thirteen, he went to work at a dry goods house in St. Louis. During the Civil War, he served as chief clerk to the provost marshal. When peace came, he started a gold-pen manufactory, and won recognition as a businessman.

At that time, a new political party was forming, the Liberal Republicans. O'Neill became a candidate for membership in the state legislature but lost by a small minority. In 1872 he was elected to the legislature by Democrats and Liberal Republicans. In 1874 and 1876 he stood with the Democrats and was reelected. During three terms in the legislature, he showed great concern for working people. He initiated laws to protect laborers on railroads by making the company liable for wages when contractors failed to pay, giving mechanics and tradesmen a lien without exception for materials furnished, exempting two hundred dollars worth of goods from taxation, and protecting married women in the control of their separate property.

O'Neill secured the enactment of a law making the public school library free. A few years later, Frederick Crunden became head of the Public Library and made its services available to all St. Louisans, not simply public school students. Crunden, incidentally, also won help from the Carnegie Foundation to erect the Central Library on Olive and two branch libraries on the Southside. O'Neill also pushed a law that provided funds annually to ensure proper reading for convicts in the jails.

In the 29th General Assembly, O'Neill promoted laws to protect servants, laborers, and mechanics in the collection of wages and to protect the poor and ignorant against dishonest employment agents. In 1882 he won a place in the United States Congress and served in the 49th, 50th, 51st, and 52nd Congress.

A handsome man with dark Irish good looks and a Grover Cleveland mustache, he gained prominence as an orator who knew well when to tell a witty story. During O'Neill's years in Congress, Henry Shaw sponsored a School of Botany at Washington University and invited William Trelease of the University of Wisconsin to direct it. When Shaw died in August 1869, Trelease became head of the Missouri Botanical Garden. He enhanced its scientific and recreational values.

A mountain in Colorado bears his name. Mount Trelease stands guard over the eastern entrance to the Eisenhower Tunnel on Interstate 70.

In the early 1890s, Congressman O'Neill took part in many memorable events. High among them was the dedication of Union Station, designed by architect Theodore Link. It was the only depot that housed all trains coming into a major city. One could go from the Atlantic Coast to the Pacific Coast without leaving this station. All trains came under one roof.

Congressman O'Neill gladly took part in the celebration in honor of Archbishop Peter Richard Kenrick's fiftieth anniversary as a bishop in 1891. Kenrick was the first prelate in America to serve a half century. The people of St. Louis gave their venerable archbishop a home on the south side of Lindell, in the second block west of Grand Avenue. Congressman O'Neill marched past Kenrick's house in the largest parade ever seen in America west of Philadelphia. Citizens gave the triangle of land across from Kenrick's new home the name Kenrick Square, a name it held until recent time.

In early 1898, Congressman O'Neill became seriously ill, and after a long period of suffering, died at Mullanphy Hospital. His wife of twenty-six years, Mary Robbins O'Neill, died a few days later. Their eight children survived them.

David R. Francis (Missouri Historical Society)

David R. Francis and Dwight Davis

Public Servants

Mayor of St. Louis, governor of Missouri, Secretary of the Interior, president of the Louisiana Purchase Exposition, and ambassador to Russia, David R. Francis played an important role in the political life of city, state, and nation for almost forty years. A member of St. Louis's "Big Cinch," a group of economic and political leaders, Francis made a fortune as a grain dealer and an official of the Mississippi Valley Trust Company, the Terminal Railroad Association, Union Electric Company, and three different street railway companies. A man of warm, handsome presence, he remained open to others.

Born in Richmond, Kentucky, and educated at a private school, he came to St. Louis to enter Washington University. He graduated with a B.A. in 1870. He lacked enough money to pursue a law degree, but he entered business with his uncle and set out to establish himself. In 1885 St. Louisans elected him mayor by 1,200 votes. He used business techniques to cut city expenses and to institute efficient administrative practices. He vetoed legislation that he deemed corrupt. In 1888 the Democratic Party nominated him as its candidate for governor, and he won. He strongly supported President Grover Cleveland, who appointed him Secretary of the Interior in 1896, the year a tornado swept across the south side of the city. After his term, Francis began to look into preparation for the World's Fair.

He lobbied for the city to be the location of the celebration of the 100th anniversary of the Louisiana Purchase. He organized the fundraising campaign to finance the celebration, and he served as president of the Board of Directors that oversaw the celebration. He felt that the city needed something like a fair. We were too self-centered. Strong and prosperous, financially we were too independent. We needed more contact with the outside world. We needed to learn something of our own merits and possibilities to keep St. Louis a great city.

The World's Fair planners selected the western section of Forest Park as the site, and leased Washington University's new campus beyond Skinker Boulevard. Governor Francis invited three hundred cultural associations to hold conventions in St. Louis in connection with the Fair. He also urged the Olympic Committee to hold its games in St. Louis. As a result, the city became the first American locale to host the international competition.

President William McKinley invited all countries of the world to take part. Fifty-five nations agreed to come. All did so except Russia, where a disastrous war with Japan had provoked domestic disorders. Japan alone sent eighty thousand specific items for display in its exhibit.

President Theodore Roosevelt, who had become president after the assassination of President McKinley and had visited the city a year before to dedicate the fair area, flicked the switch in Washington, D.C., which set the electric lights ablaze in Forest Park. Ten thousand flags soared from towers, domes, and flagstaffs. John Philip Sousa raised his baton for the World's Fair Hymn. The fourteen palaces, featuring subjects such as education, agriculture, and transportation, provided five million square feet of exhibit space, with six million more square feet available for outdoor exhibits. Fifteen hundred and seventy-six buildings spread out over the area.

Other fairs had stressed finished products. The St. Louis Fair featured processes. The visitors saw jewelers and rope-makers at work. Miners from Montana compared methods with their counterparts from Sweden.

As a visitor walked down the central walkway called the "Pike," he could eat new food creations, the ice cream cone and the "hot dog," and drink tea cooled by ice, another novel concoction. He could climb an Alp, take a ride to view the city on a 260-foot high Ferris Wheel, walk the Rocky Road to Dublin, and hear tenor John McCormack on his way to world fame. He could talk to Geronimo, the once-feared Apache warrior. President Theodore Roosevelt spoke with the chief, in fact, during the last days of the Fair after his reelection in November 1904. The president invited Geronimo to ride in the inaugural parade the following March. The Apache chieftain agreed to do so.

Exactly 19,694,855 individuals visited that greatest of fairs. In looking back, they noted these distinct qualities of the exposition: the interest in other cultures, the Victorian tone of the entertainment, the stressing of processes rather than of products, the applications of science, the emphasis on the brotherhood of man, and the association of so many people in such a friendly way.

The Louisiana Purchase Exposition Company restored the park, designated the Art Palace a city museum, moved several statues, and built the Jefferson Memorial as a permanent library and museum on Lindell Boulevard.

The wide challenge of Governor Francis to other agencies to give attention to the Fair offered the new president of Saint Louis University, Father William Banks Rogers, an opportunity to bring the school back into the mainstream. In the previous fifty years, it had fallen from its great status in the 1840s and early '50s to a standstill, while Washington University and Christian Brothers College and several other colleges in the area of St. Louis flourished.

Father Rogers accepted Governor Francis's invitation and placed a booth in the Palace of Education. Along with six other local enterprisers, he took a full-page advertisement in the World's Fair Guide. He welcomed a board of advisors that included Julius Walsh, Festus Wade, Richard Kearns, August Schlafly, David Walker, and others. A short time later these men supported the new archbishop, John J. Glennon, in his hopes and plans for a new cathedral.

After the Fair, Governor Francis continued to serve his country, ending his great public career as ambassador to Russia at the time of the Bolshevik Revolution.

Like Governor Francis, Dwight F. Davis divided time between local and overseas service to his country. Unlike Francis, who had to work to wealth, Davis grew up in Portland Place and attended Harvard University. A tall, lithe, graceful man, he was a star left-handed tennis player there, and with his partner won the national championship. He championed an international trophy for tennis and competed internationally himself. Eventually, the trophy gained the name the Davis Cup.

Dwight Davis, at home on the tennis court.

In 1914 and 1915 he became commissioner of the city's Department of Parks and Recreation. He removed many "Keep Off the Grass" signs to promote participating sports—baseball and soccer—among ordinary citizens and neighborhood teams. He authorized the opening of tennis courts in several city parks. These were the first public tennis courts in the country.

Inter-park tennis matches followed, then baseball and soccer. The Ben Millers, the Carondelet Sunday Morning Club, and the Kutis Mortuary sponsored teams. A St. Louisan, Harry Ratican, became recognized as the best soccer player in the country during the days of World War I. Even Tower Grove Park, a "Victorian strolling park" under Director Bernice Gurney but not under the Department of Parks, followed with clay and artificially surfaced courts, a wading pool for youngsters nearby, and corkball backstops along Arsenal Street.

A lieutenant colonel in the Missouri Guard, Dwight Davis won the Distinguished Service Cross during World War I. After the conflict, President Calvin Coolidge named him Secretary of War, and later President Herbert Hoover appointed him Governor General of the Philippines.

Several years ago, the city named courts in Forest Park near the Jefferson Memorial the Davis Courts. Tennis stars from many countries played there, including Chuck McKinley, St. Louis's own Wimbledon champion, and Ken Rosewall of Australia.

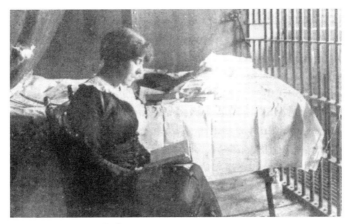

Fannie Mooney Sellins

Social Reformers
Sellins, Dempsey,
Kenkel

E arly in the last century, St. Louis had three great social reformers: Fannie Mooney Sellins worked for the right of labor to organize; Father Tim Dempsey looked to the downtrodden and depressed at a time when government had not yet reached a sense of responsibility for its disadvantaged citizens; and Frederick Kenkel, organizer and editor, led the way toward proper facing the social problems the times presented.

Fannie Mooney Sellins,
Labor Organizer

I n most areas early in the twentieth century, men presumed the right to organize. They set up social clubs, golf clubs, automobile clubs, and saw the need for doctors, farmers, and business-men to organize. But somehow, the average American never accepted the right of laboring men to organize. Even today, in this century of freedom, most of our southern and western states have laws against unionization.

Hours were long, wages were low, manage-ment ignored the basic rules of safety, fire escapes were inadequate, and facilities unsanitary. Workers lacked security, and they depended entirely on their wages. Police protected the property of the owners but cared little for the needs of the workers. Courts favored big business, even while legislators ruled in favor of labor. Laboring people languished powerless against their bosses.

One industry in particular that was having difficulties was the garment workers' union. The entire nation realized the awful conditions in 1911 at the Triangle Shirtwaist Company in New York, when a fire incinerated 146 women workers, mostly teenagers. In St. Louis, several years before that terrible fire, hundreds of women workers labored in equally poor conditions at Marks & Haas Clothing on Washington Avenue.

In 1907, when the work week was fifty-four hours and the wage was five dollars a week, the leader of the garment workers was Fannie Mooney Sellins, a widow with several children. She worked for the firm of Marks & Haas, on the southeast corner of Thirteenth and Washington, which locked out hundreds of its employees of

Locals 23 and 67 of the United Garment Workers Association. The women workers, many of whom did not speak English, worked fifty hours a week, nine hours a day Monday through Friday and five hours on Saturday. The standard wage at that time was nine dollars a week. One worker complained that high-speed machines shattered nerves in a few years. The company ignored safety rules. In one year, for instance, five hundred minor accidents occurred, chiefly to fingers caught by needles and in machines. The management was trying to destroy the local garment workers' union and institute an open shop. The lockout notice went out in English, Jewish, Italian, and Slavic languages. The women struck in response. Marks & Haas hired the Matthew Kiely Detective Agency. They brought in strikebreakers from New York and Chicago.

When Fannie Mooney Sellins took charge of the labor union at the death of her predecessor, Hannah Hennessey, she went around the country telling union wives to boycott Marks' clothes. It proved so successful that by October 11, 1910, following two weeks of negotiations, Marks & Haas signed a closed shop agreement, with wage issues to be settled by negotiations or, if necessary, by third-party arbitration. Fannie Mooney next moved on Schwab Company on Market Street, but in the meantime, the central office of the United Garment Workers Association vetoed Fannie's efforts to use her method in the future. The UGWA rejected Fannie's efforts because of the Danbury Hatters case, in which the Supreme Court had ruled a secondary boycott unconstitutional. At this time, the United Mine Workers asked her to be an organizer, so she went east, was thrown in jail for picketing on one occasion, and even the president of the United States, Woodrow Wilson, couldn't get her out of jail.

Eventually, she was released, and at the end of World War I, she picketed a mine where violence broke out. A hired guard pushed Fannie, an unarmed woman. As she ran for the safety of Constantin Rafalko's backyard, three hired gunmen shot her in the back—a horrible deed, against the code of any cold-blooded gunman of the West. A nephew of Rafalko saw the shooting. No judge sentenced her murderers. Instead, the jury ruled that the deputies had acted in self-defense and denounced "the alien or foreign agitators who instill Anarchy and Bolshevist Doctrines into the minds of un-American and uneducated Aliens." If it wasn't for Rose Feuer, a historian today who keeps alive the memory of Fannie Mooney in the area of St. Louis, she would have been forgotten. She should not be.

Fair treatment was slow in coming. In the 1920s, powerless "company unions" prevailed in industry, but the New Deal finally changed the pattern with the Wagner Act of 1935 that protected the workers' right to organize.

Monsignor Timothy Dempsey,
Father of the Poor

While Fannie Mooney Sellins worked with unions to improve labor conditions, Father Timothy Dempsey organized relief for the down-trodden when government offered none. A native of Ireland, Timothy Dempsey became a priest of the Archdiocese of St. Louis in 1891. Seven years later, Archbishop Glennon assigned him to St. Patrick's, the oldest Irish parish in St. Louis, at Sixth and Biddle.

By this time, Poles, Liths, Italians, Bohemians, and Slovaks also worshipped at St. Patricks. Most of the Irish had moved west, first to St. Lawrence O'Toole and then to St. Theresa's and other parishes. Father Tim opened a hotel for working men in 1906. He welcomed the homeless. In the winter of 1907, the hotel welcomed nearly ten thousand guests. In 1910 he began a day nursery. In 1911 he started a hotel for working women, and in 1922 a home for African American workers. He purchased a large plot in Calvary Cemetery called "Exiles Rest" for his "boys."

Asked to mediate strikes, he was surprisingly successful. Returning veterans from World War I found little help from the government. They had served overseas, and many engaged in gang wars in St. Louis. The Hogans and the Eagans engaged in shootouts. Father Dempsey worked for peace, and

Father Timothy Dempsey

the once-gangsters became creative citizens, several of them even rising in state politics. Father Tim organized a popular boys' band, featured on the front cover of David Losos's pictorial booklet, *The Irish in St. Louis.*

A stout, friendly man with an appealing personality, Father Tim made friends everywhere. Historian Harold McAuliffe wrote his biography in the 1930s.

Frederick P. Kenkel, Social Theorist

While Fannie Mooney worked to build unions and Father Tim Dempsey provided relief for the desperate, Frederick Kenkel analyzed social conditions and pointed out ways to improve them.

In 1905, at the age of twenty-two, already a seasoned journalist with experience in business and management, Kenkel had come to St. Louis and accepted the editorship of *Amerika*, a respected German daily. He soon became the key figure in the *Central Verein*, the most influential German-Catholic organization in the country. From 1908 onward, his personal career was closely tied to the Catholic life of a large segment of the German-American community.

Frederick Kenkel

In 1914 Europe began its first general war in a century. The internationally known St. Louis editor, William Marion Reedy, had opposed American ventures in the Pacific in the 1890s. Consistently, in 1914, he opposed embroiling the country in Europe's latest war. In both houses of Congress, individuals said, "No." Congressman William T. Igoe of St. Louis's Northside voted against the declaration of war in 1917. The people reelected him during the struggle in 1918.

Editor Kenkel received a threatening letter from a writer who identified himself only as "one who knows." He obviously didn't know that Kenkel had two sons in uniform. One was wounded. *Amerika* and other German-Catholic publications had their mailing privileges temporarily suspended. St. Louisan Kate Richards O'Hare, the Socialist editor of *National Rip-Saw*, as American as President Woodrow Wilson himself, suffered more. The government sentenced her to the federal penitentiary in Atlanta for a remark that the nation was sending Dakota farm boys to be cannon fodder for the Kaiser's guns. Her letters about conditions in Atlanta brought about prison reform, and brought her just honors.

A vitriolic paper, *The Menace*, attacked the members of the *Central Verein* as "a bunch of traitors who deserved deportation to Germany."

Actually, their ancestors had come to America as refugees from German militarism.

Hostilities ceased on November 11, 1918. Two months later, in January 1919, Prohibition became the law of the land, with the ratification of the Eighteenth Amendment to the United States Constitution by the required number of states. The vote closed the breweries. St. Louisans turned to home brew.

Before the war, America had welcomed immigrants. The newspapers featured the customs and costumes of the newcomers. Now the government put quotas on the number of immigrants. Newspapers and magazines denounced foreign languages and customs. They ruled out the terms German-American, Irish-American, Polish-American, and other "hyphenated Americans." Editors stressed the fact that all were Americans. The American population no longer resembled a "salad bowl." It was becoming a "melting pot."

The postwar period in America was a time of readjustment, over-expansion of farm production, anti-union court decisions, and unemployment. The St. Louis white community, however, did not face the high rate of unemployment that other groups did, especially unskilled African Americans who had moved to St. Louis from the rural South to take menial jobs in wartime. But the general uncertainty affected all people. The government had no solutions to economic problems and no programs for returning veterans.

During those postwar years, Frederick Kenkel revitalized the *Central Verein*. He Anglicized the name to the Central Bureau for Social Justice and worked for the benefit of all. His main concern was the proper organization of economic life according to the principles of Pius XI's encyclical of 1931, *Quadragesimo Anno*. He published a highly respected magazine, *The Social Justice Review*, the first Catholic journal to make social reform its main issue. It drew praise from the leading Catholic social spokesman of the time, Msgr. John A. Ryan of Catholic University and the National Catholic Welfare Conference.

At home, Kenkel promoted institutions of social help, such as credit unions and cooperatives. He supported the National Catholic Rural Life Conference and continually urged the widest possible distribution of productive property.

Annie Malone. Photograph by Leorna L. Lee of an undated portrait by an unidentified artist. (Annie Malone Children and Family Service Center)

Annie Malone

Entrepreneur and Philanthropist

Race relations in St. Louis were never ideal. The *Plessy v. Ferguson* decision of 1896 set back efforts to improve conditions of African Americans in St. Louis, and these conditions grew worse with the influx of unskilled workers from the South at the time of World War I and World War II. During the Depression, unemployment or under-employment among African Americans soared to 80 percent.

Annie Turnbo Malone broke this pattern. Born at Metropolis in southern Illinois in 1869 and orphaned early, Annie, a sickly child, moved to Peoria with her older siblings and periodically attended high school. While there, she discovered an affinity for chemistry. She recognized the potential market of beauty products for African American women. Her skill with chemical composites played a critical role in the development of her hair-strengthening formula. In 1902, she moved to St. Louis and patented her product, Poro, in 1906. She married a man named Pope in

1903. After they divorced, she married Aaron Malone, a school principal, in 1914.

Annie found immediate success in St. Louis with a door-to-door sales campaign. Her true success, however, was in her decision to franchise her product. She trained women to franchise the product across the country, the most notable being her future competitor, Madame C. J. Walker. Her hair business eventually had thirty-two branches.

By 1917 she was worth well over a million dollars, and she opened Poro College, a multipurpose facility that included a beauty operator's training school, a five hundred-seat auditorium, a roof garden, several committee rooms, and an elegant dining room. She brought black entertainers of prominence here, such as Marian Anderson, Roland Hayes, and Ethel Waters. They performed on the stage of Poro College. She helped Howard University in Washington. By 1924 she was a multimillionaire and drove a Rolls Royce. In 1930 she moved Poro headquarters to Chicago but continued her St. Louis charities. The St. Louis Colored Orphans Home was renamed the Annie Malone Children's Home in 1946. Annie had donated land for the home. Other charities and organizations that she gave generously to included Howard University, Wilberforce University, the YMCA, and St. James A.M.E. Church.

During her years, African Americans made slow but steady advances in St. Louis. Sadly,

Homer G. Phillips, a prominent black lawyer, was assassinated. Rather than setting back the racial improvement, this act stirred positive action. Above all, people like Annie Malone did so much for the general improvement of their community. She was the first self-made woman millionaire in America.

Annie Malone's legacy is alive and well in the Ville neighborhood in St. Louis City. The Annie Malone Children and Family Service Center, located on Annie Malone Drive, continues the community-improvement mission that Malone's generosity helped to create. Community growth is dependent on the support and generosity of its leaders, and as a business leader, Annie Malone not only offered assistance through her charities, but she also offered opportunity in employment through her company and college.

Judge Nathan B. Young

Judge Nathan B. Young

Racial Pathfinder

Judge Nathan B. Young—jurist, editor, artist, local historian of the St. Louis black community—was instrumental in founding and operating the *St. Louis American* and is the author of "Your St. Louis and Mine," a history of the St. Louis black community published in 1937.

Nathan Young was born in Tuskegee, Alabama, where his father was a teacher of English. Later, his father became head of the English Department at Georgia State College and then at Florida A&M in Tallahassee. Nathan himself graduated from Florida A&M, went to Yale University in New Haven, and finished law school in 1918. He came to St. Louis in 1924, when his father moved to Missouri to become president of Lincoln University. Nathan entered the practice of law in St. Louis.

In 1929 the Depression hit. Although St. Louis, with its many diversified industries, was not hit as hard as one-industry citics like Pittsburgh and Detroit, unskilled African Americans who had moved in from the South during World War I for war work were especially hard-hit. At that time, Young began building the new newspaper, the *St. Louis American*, as editorial writer and manager. The paper was especially anxious in promoting the cause of laboring men such as the Pullman car porters, led by J. Philips Randolph, a scarcely remembered but important part of the labor movement.

Young recognized the importance of the black music tradition in St. Louis and traced it to the German music tradition. "All our famous black musicians, among them Tom Turpin and Scott Joplin," he pointed out, "went to German music teachers to get their formal education. W. C. Handy tells us that he got his basic music training from a man of German background named Bach."

St. Louis, Judge Young pointed out, had been to the Supreme Court on civil rights in six different cases. Everyone knows of the *Dred Scott* decision. Even before, the status of African Americans proved a major issue when the state was admitted to the Union in 1821.

St. Louis took strides ahead immediately after World War II, when, thanks to the inspiring talk of Father Claude Heithaus, Saint Louis University became the first university in a former slave state to integrate. Not long afterwards, a new arch-bishop, Joseph Elmer Ritter, called attention to the Catholic tradition that every person must worship in his own parish. He thus broke down the parish

segregation, worked against neighborhood segregation, and integrated 259 schools. This action had
its effect on the decision of the Supreme Court a
few years later in *Brown v. Topeka*.

In the meantime, Judge Nathan Young himself
had become the first black city court judge in
St. Louis City. A few years later, not just members
of the aldermanic council, but mayors, were black.
The first black congressman from Missouri,
William Clay, was elected by the North District of
St. Louis to the national Congress.

Oliver Lafayette Parks

Oliver Lafayette Parks

Pioneer of the Air Age

O liver Lafayette Parks, a Chevrolet salesman turned school founder, beat the Depression. No graduate of his school was ever out of work, in spite of bad times. He prepared many men as pilots and mechanics for civil aviation and the United States Air Force in World War II.

A native of northern Illinois, Parks was a successful automobile salesman in St. Louis. His hobby was aviation when flying was for the "Crazies." He himself allegedly welcomed his favorite Cubs to Sportsman's Park on one occasion by circling the flagpole in center field. Then his friend, Charles "Slim" Lindbergh, who flew the mail from St. Louis to Chicago, changed views on aviation by flying nonstop from New York to Paris in a Ryan monoplane, the *Spirit of St. Louis*. Lindbergh became a hero, flying became a reasonable occupation, and Parks became a school founder.

Denied a dealership by the Chevrolet people, he gave up selling cars to selling spaces in a flight school he intended to start. Two years later, he bought property in the Cahokia Bottoms near the historic Church of the Holy Family and opened his school there. Everyone who would be a pilot or a future mechanic had to go through the full routine, shoveling coal, putting out landing lights at night, sweeping the classrooms. Property Supervisor Henry Schnitger saw to it that all measured up. Parks mechanics and aeronautic engineers as well as pilots outclassed the trainees at other schools.

The Depression came in 1929, but Parks carried on. In 1934, Jimmy Doolittle asked Parks mechanics to tune up his plane and streamline the fuselage. He set a speed record for men. Louise Thaden flew faster than any other woman, setting the record at Parks. All great aviators came to take advantage of the skill of Parks mechanics in tuning up their planes. Eddie Rickenbacker, Roscoe Turner, Lady Mary Heath—every well-known pilot came to Parks. All the while, beginning in 1935, Hitler began to build the German air force, defying the Versailles Treaty that forbade Germany from having military planes. Would-be German aviators had trained in gliders. Britain relied on its navy, and France on its Maginot Line. Parks led the world.

In 1939, Hitler sent his troops into Poland, then in the spring to Denmark, Norway, Belgium, and France. Major General "Hap" Arnold called flight school directors to a meeting. The Army Air Corps needed trained men, pilots and mechanics, but could not pay them.

Only Parks, the risk-taker, agreed. He did more than open his school to military personnel. He borrowed money to expand in other locations. He had to call on his best sales techniques to win new investors.

War came with Pearl Harbor, and our Air Force was ready, and Parks had a great hand in that readiness. After the war he affiliated his school with Saint Louis University, to the advantage of both institutions.

Congresswoman Leonor K. Sullivan

Leonor K. Sullivan

Consumers Advocate

L eonor Kretzer Sullivan, the first woman to serve Missouri in the House of Representatives, represented the Third District of South St. Louis from 1952 to 1977. Born in southwest St. Louis, she attended public and private schools and took night courses at Washington University. In 1941 she joined the League of Women Voters. On December 27 of that year, she married John B. Sullivan, who had just won a seat in the 77th Congress. Mrs. Sullivan served as an aide to her husband during the 77th and 78th Congress from 1941 to 1947, and then in the 81st and 82nd, from January 1949 until his death two years later. Mrs. Sullivan ran for the seat of her late husband in 1953 and won over five Democrat rivals and overwhelmed the Republican opponent. The South Side voters elected her to the 83rd Congress and reelected her for eleven more terms, until 1977, when she declined to run again. To the other congressional chamber, Missouri sent two outstanding St. Louisans, Tom

Eagleton and John Danforth, a pair no state could equal at the time.

In the 1950s, she waged a five-year battle to win approval for a plan to bring government surplus food to the needy, which finally became a law in 1959. She was the principal architect/author of the 1968 Credit Protection Act. President Lyndon Johnson gave her special recognition for her part in its passage. Over the years, she became known as a consumers' advocate, especially for product labeling and meat inspection. She cosponsored the Equal Rights Act of 1963, but, like Carrie Chapman Catt, the architect of the Women's Suffrage Amendment, she saw the good and the bad in the Equal Rights Amendment and was the only woman to vote against it.

While concerned with the big issues of government, she could still respond to personal concerns of ordinary citizens of St. Louis, among them writers and photographers. When architect Ted Wofford released his feasibility study of St. Joseph's Shrine in the Near North Side, she supported the successful drive to preserve it. A lifelong fan of the Mississippi River, she found her home on the bluff overlooking the river on South Broadway. She promoted flood control projects and river safety bills. She was a driving force behind legislation that supported construction of the Jefferson National Expansion Memorial, the famous Gateway Arch on the riverfront. She stood with mayors James Conway, A. J. Cervantes, and former mayor Raymond Tucker at the placement of the final triangle uniting the north and south legs of the monument.

During her years in public life, St. Louis had many mayors—Alois P. Kaufmann, Joseph Darst, Raymond Tucker, A. J. Cervantes, John Poelker, James Conway, and Vincent Schoemehl. The Federal Highway Program developed during those years. Pope John XXIII named Archbishop Ritter a cardinal of the Church. He took an active part in most forward thrusts of the Vatican Council, such as religious liberty and the apostolate of the laity, to the joy of Sullivan and her constituents.

The long-serving president of Saint Louis University, Father Paul C. Reinert, was able to keep the university at its mid-city location with the help of Mrs. Harriet Fordyce. She financed expansion east of Grand in an area where her father, General Daniel Frost, had mustered his unit of the state militia in May 1861.

During Sullivan's years in office, a treasure of her district, the Missouri Botanical Garden, gave up any plans to move to Franklin County. Professor Raymond Tucker's anti-smoke campaign of the 1930s made this possible. The Garden gained new vitality with the leadership of John Lehman as head of the Friends of the Garden. Director Fritz Wendt authorized the Climatron, the first geodesic-dome conservatory. Dr. Peter Raven brought the Garden to a new plateau of greatness with the addition of the Ridgeway Center, the

English Woodland Garden, and the Japanese Garden. At the same time, John Karel revitalized Tower Grove Park.

Mrs. Sullivan attended the reception in honor of Archbishop Joseph L. Ritter on the occasion of Pope John XXIII's naming Ritter a cardinal of the Church. She welcomed the new vision the Second Vatican Council gave to the Church.

Also during her years, there was tremendous advance made locally in the race issues. The Homer G. Phillips Hospital, named for a St. Louis lawyer who had worked in the interests of race improvement, became one of the leading hospitals of the country. With top-flight medical schools at Washington University and at Saint Louis University, the city became a major health center. Washington University reached a high level among American universities. The president of Saint Louis University turned the mid-town campus from a constellation of parking lots and crowded buildings into a spacious mid-city park, and pledged the school to leadership among Catholic universities.

Two historians, graduates of Saint Louis University, became presidents of other local universities—Dr. Arlen Dykstra at Missouri Baptist University, and Dr. Blanche Touhill at the University of Missouri–St. Louis. Dr. Dykstra guided his institution in a strong, balanced Christian spirit, when so many other once-Christian schools were watering down their Christian heritage in the name of diversity. Dr. Touhill wrote the history of her school, arranged for a program of Irish studies that won international recognition, and provided space for the prestigious Mercantile Library. The Blanche Touhill Center for the Arts keeps her memory alive on the campus and in the educational world at large.

While much direct influence was felt in Sullivan's own South Side Third District, her interests and concerns had benefited the entire St. Louis area. In 1983 a grateful citizenry honored her by refurbishing Wharf Street and renaming it "Leonor K. Sullivan Boulevard."

Bob Burnes

Bob Broeg
and Bob Burnes

Sportswriters

F rom the end of World War II to the end of
the Cold War, Bob Burnes and Bob Broeg
kept St. Louisans aware of what went on
here and elsewhere in the world of sport. It was a
time of great joy for St. Louis fans, as the Cardinals
repeatedly went into the World Series and came
out victorious, and the Hawks and the Bills were
national champions in basketball. Soccer was a
highly successful St. Louis sport, especially at Saint
Louis University and in the World Cup of 1950,
and St. Louis posted one Wimbledon champion.
And the two Bobs told it all. Sometimes Broeg
would be writing as a feverish fan rather than an
analyzing sportswriter.

Burnes was born in the northwest part of the
city, attended CBC and Saint Louis U, and reflected
the interests of those institutions. Broeg grew up
in southeast St. Louis, attended Cleveland High
and the University of Missouri, and had special

Bob Broeg

place in his roomy heart for the Missouri Tigers on the court and on the gridiron.

Bob Burnes was a sportswriter for the *St. Louis Globe-Democrat* and pioneered as a sportscaster on the nation's first open-line radio program over KMOX, beginning in the 1950s and going until the 1980s. He also wrote for the Sporting News and spoke at hundreds of Communion breakfasts. The son of Brian Burnes, president of the St. Louis Soccer Association, Bob welcomed the World Cup team of 1950 and the Billiken champions of Bob Goelker and Harry Keough.

Broeg was sports editor of the *St. Louis Post-Dispatch* for many years and became assistant to the publisher in 1980. He ran a weekly column in the paper and had a weekly show on KMOX. He published more than twenty books, among them *The Hundred Greatest Moments in St. Louis Sports*. Later in his career, he tended to look back and tell of the great days of the past rather than tell what went on locally in the various high schools and other areas. Broeg's steel-trap mind was a fountain of knowledge to sportswriters and fans alike, telling tales of Brownie and Cardinal lore. Burnes, however, was extremely concerned with what went on in the high schools and inter-park competition in tennis, soccer, baseball— whatever it might be. If you wanted to find out when the Y would have its next ski trip, Bob Burnes would carry that.

A family man, Bob Burnes and his wife, Adele, had four daughters, four granddaughters, two grandsons, a great-granddaughter, and a great grandson. Broeg had a small family.

In Burnes's column one was more likely to learn about the longstanding rivalry between Saint Louis University High School and CBC. In Broeg's column one would hear about the career of George Sisler—the Browns' great Sizzler—who batted over .400 three different years, back before the big war. Bob Burnes's trademark was his ever-present cigar, which evoked many pleasantries. Bob Broeg's trademark was his grin and his little bow tie. Broeg was a little more demonstrative in meeting people, instantly becoming great friends with anyone willing to talk sports, especially about his boyhood idol, Frankie Frisch.

The number of honors Broeg won over the years is awesome. Among them, he was on the Board of Directors of the National Baseball Hall of Fame and, in 1957, the Hall of Fame of the National Sportscasters and Sportswriters Association. He was elected to the National Baseball Hall of Fame in 1980.

Every season, both Bobs predicted the Cardinals were going to win, even when facts might suggest a poor year. In fact, they reflected the attitude of the bulk of Cardinal fans, who brooked no criticism of their beloved Redbirds.

If there was a valid criticism of the two Bobs, it was that they were public relations men for the

Cardinals rather than critics of the team or analysts of the play. They never second-guessed manager or umpire. Any other criticism might be that they did not give hockey and other sports the same warm attention that they gave baseball, although Bob Burnes was always strong for basketball and soccer with his beloved Bills and Broeg concerned his musings about Missouri's basketball and football programs.

They recorded a happier sports scene than we see today, when star athletes were neighbors and fellow parishioners, intent on winning the championship this year, and not transient millionaires worried about next year's salary.

Dr. Walter Ehrlich

Dr. Walter Ehrlich

Teacher-Historian

D r. Walter Erlich, the author of *Zion in the Valley*, a book that won national acclaim as a definitive, two-volume history of the Jewish community in St. Louis, taught for many years at University City and Horton-Watkins Ladue high schools and at the University of Missouri–St. Louis. He was born in the immigrant neighborhood on the near north side, at 1812 Carr Street, a few blocks north of Delmar and west of Tucker Boulevard. He attended Soldan High School and served his country in the U.S. Army during World War II in the Pacific.

After returning to the states from service in 1946, Walter married his college sweetheart, Sylvia. He won his first teaching position at University City High School. His salary in the beginning was $2,600 a year. That one year he signed up for turned into eleven. Dr. Erlich was principal of the Shaare Emeth religious school and was active in United Hebrew, Shaare Jedek, and Central Reform congregations. He served on the

Board of Trustees of the *St. Louis Jewish Light*. He took part in community history organizations such at the Greater St. Louis Historical Society. He gave lectures. He published a book in 1974 called *Presidential Impeachment: An American Dilemma*, which came out just before the Watergate scandal and was a runaway seller until the resignation of President Nixon.

After winning his Ph.D. in History at Washington University in St. Louis, he taught for many years at the University of Missouri–St. Louis. While there, he decided to undertake the needed study of the Jewish community in St. Louis. He published *Zion in the Valley*. Several reviewers, including the *St. Louis Jewish Light*, applauded it as the definitive history of the Jewish community.

While an expert on local history, and especially of his own people in St. Louis, he kept his students interested in the wider picture. He had written his dissertation, not on something specifically dealing with local Jewish history, but on the famous *Dred Scott* decision. He also stressed the importance of teaching Western Civilization so that there was no overemphasis on the local ethnic community.

The story he told of his ethnic group showed a people becoming more and more an integral part of the St. Louis community. Some of them, especially the Eastern European Jewish people, rose from a limited scope to extreme activity in the entire community. Many of his fellow Jewish people were highly active in promoting community activities of all kinds: the Symphony, art work, health care with Wohl Clinic and the Jewish Hospital (Barnes-Jewish later, after affiliation), the Steinberg Ice Rink in Forest Park, and Simon Recreational Centers at several universities. The Roscoe and Wilma Messing Award in Literature brought nationally distinguished writers to Saint Louis University, among them Barbara Tuchman and James Michener.

In his late years, Dr. Erlich completed a detailed autobiography, *The Saga of Walter Ehrlich*. He wrote it in his distinctive, clear, and smooth-flowing style. It is warmly personal and yet done with the discipline of a nationally respected historian. In addition to his wife of sixty years, four children, all active in the academic world, survived him.

Epilogue

The reader has looked at the origin and growth of St. Louis through the eyes of interesting individuals, some front-page personalities, others low-key achievers; some widely known, some overlooked by historians. He could view the many facets of the city's growth and development:

1) its totally unique origin as a French settlement in a predominantly English-speaking region;

2) its growth in colonial times as the merchandising center of the midcontinent;

3) its easy transition from a European colony to an American territory;

4) its welcome of Irish and German immigrants, unwanted in English-speaking regions;

5) its location as western military focus, with Jefferson Barracks as the hub;

6) its religious development under three bishops: W. V. DuBourg from France, Joseph Rosati from Italy, and Peter Richard Kenrick from Ireland—the latter becoming the first archbishop of the midcontinent in 1847;

7) its troubles in a politically divided border area during the Civil War;

8) its rise to prominence among American cities, once peace came;

9) its policy of gradual Americanization for new immigrants from Eastern Europe, who contributed greatly to the city's development;

10) its twentieth-century history resembled that of others!

About the Author

Over the past forty years, Father William Barnaby Faherty, S.J., has received invitations to write the story of the most important botanical garden in the world and its founder, Henry Shaw; of the most influential flight school and its chief, Oliver Lafayette Parks; of space exploration at NASA's installation in Florida; of the St. Louis archdiocese; and of the city of St. Louis itself. *St. Louis: A Concise History*, co-authored with neighborhood specialist NiNi Harris, is in its fourth edition.

Following the advice of one of his mentors, Pulitzer Prize-winner Paul Horgan, Faherty tried his hand several times with fiction. MGM adapted his first novel, *A Wall for San Sebastian*, for a movie. His third novel, *The Call of Pope Octavian*, tells of a future pope who updates the administrative machinery of the Papacy as Vatican II has updated external attitudes. The Missouri Writers' Guild has rated several of his books the best work of the year.

His *St. Louis Irish: An Unmatched Celtic Community* went into its fourth printing, and his recently published *The St. Louis German Catholics* is nearing its second printing.

A native of St. Louis of Irish-Alsatian ancestry, Father Faherty received a Doctor of Philosophy degree in History at Saint Louis University in 1949. Rockhurst University conferred on him an honorary Doctorate in Humane Letters in 1993.